Living things need water

Bobbie Kalman

🌲 **Crabtree Publishing Company**

www.crabtreebooks.com

Introducing Living Things

Created by Bobbie Kalman

Dedicated by Crystal Sikkens
To Nancy and Rich, all the best in your new life together.

**Author and
Editor-in-Chief**
Bobbie Kalman

Editors
Reagan Miller
Robin Johnson

Photo research
Crystal Sikkens

Design
Bobbie Kalman
Katherine Kantor
Samantha Crabtree (cover)

Production coordinator
Katherine Kantor

Illustrations
Barbara Bedell: pages 14 (shark and whale), 15 (all except sea turtle),
  24 (liquid, plants, and river)
Bonna Rouse: pages 14 (sea turtle), 15 (sea turtle), 24 (pond)
Margaret Amy Salter: pages 10, 14 (octopus), 24 (ocean)

Photographs
© Fotolia.com: page 24 (ice)
© iStockphoto.com: pages 5 (bottom right), 16, 17
© ShutterStock.com: front cover, back cover, pages 1, 3, 4, 5 (top), 6,
  7 (all except seal), 8, 9, 10, 11, 12, 13, 14, 15, 18, 19, 20, 21, 22, 23,
  24 (clouds, dew, lake, and rain)
Other images by Creatas and Digital Vision

Library and Archives Canada Cataloguing in Publication

Kalman, Bobbie, 1947-
    Living things need water / Bobbie Kalman.

(Introducing living things)
Includes index.
ISBN 978-0-7787-3232-7 (bound).--ISBN 978-0-7787-3256-3 (pbk.)

    1. Water--Juvenile literature. 2. Hydrologic cycle--Juvenile
literature. 3. Plant-water relationships--Juvenile literature. 4. Animal-
water relationships--Juvenile literature. I. Title. II. Series.

GB662.3.K33 2007   j571   C2007-904242-2

Library of Congress Cataloging-in-Publication Data

Kalman, Bobbie.
  Living things need water / Bobbie Kalman.
    p. cm. -- (Introducing living things)
  Includes index.
  ISBN-13: 978-0-7787-3232-7 (rlb)
  ISBN-10: 0-7787-3232-0 (rlb)
  ISBN-13: 978-0-7787-3256-3 (pb)
  ISBN-10: 0-7787-3256-8 (pb)
  1. Water--Juvenile literature. 2. Hydrologic cycle--Juvenile literature.
3. Plant-water relationships--Juvenile literature. 4. Animal-water
relationships--Juvenile literature. I. Title. II. Series.

GB662.3.K353 2007
571--dc22
                                                    2007027225

Crabtree Publishing Company

www.crabtreebooks.com   1-800-387-7650

**Published in Canada
Crabtree Publishing**
616 Welland Ave.
St. Catharines, Ontario
L2M 5V6

**Published in the United States
Crabtree Publishing**
PMB16A
350 Fifth Ave., Suite 3308
New York, NY 10118

**Published in the United Kingdom
Crabtree Publishing**
White Cross Mills
High Town, Lancaster
LA1 4XS

**Published in Australia
Crabtree Publishing**
386 Mt. Alexander Rd.
Ascot Vale (Melbourne)
VIC 3032

Contents

What is water?

Water is a **liquid**. Water has no taste. Water has no color. Water has no smell. Water has no shape.

Water is everywhere. Water is in rivers and lakes.

Water is in oceans.

Water is in ponds.

5

Water changes

Rain is liquid water. It falls from the sky in drops. Rain makes things wet. This girl is wet from the rain. Rain helps plants grow. Plants need water.

There is water in clouds.
When it is warm, the water
falls as rain. When it is cold,
the water falls as snow.

a snowflake

Ice and snow are **solid**
water. In winter, animals
eat snow to get the water
they need.

Dew is liquid water.
Small animals, such as this
insect, get water from dew.

7

Living things

People are living
things. Plants are
living things. Animals
are living things.

Water is not a living
thing, but all living
things need water
to stay alive.

Living things are made mostly of water. There is water inside your body. There is water inside plants. There is water inside animals. Most living things need to drink water every day.

Thirsty plants

Plants need water to grow and make new plants. They need water to make food. Plants take in water through their **roots**. Most plant roots are in **soil**. There is water in soil. These plants are growing in soil beside a river. They get plenty of water.

roots

Plants make food in their leaves. They make food from sunlight, air, and water. Plants cannot make food without water.

This plant is growing in soil. Its roots take water from the soil. The water travels up the stem to the leaves.

These plants are growing in water. Their roots take in the water the plants need. The water travels up the stems.

How do they drink?

People and animals also need water to grow. They need water to move. People and animals feel thirsty when they need water. How do they drink water?

People and many animals drink water using their mouths.

Some animals do not have mouths. Birds drink water using their beaks. Some insects use a **proboscis** to eat and drink. An elephant has a proboscis, too. It is called a **trunk**!

Birds use their beaks to drink water.

proboscis

Elephants suck up water with their trunks and squirt it into their mouths.

13

Living in oceans

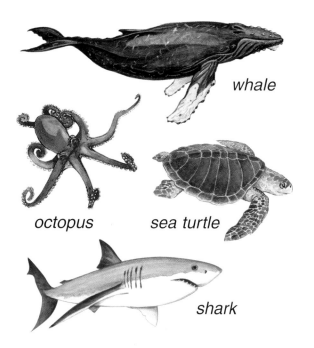

whale

octopus

sea turtle

shark

Many animals live in water. They cannot live on land. Water is their home. Water has all the food they need, too. Sharks, whales, octopuses, sea turtles, and many kinds of fish live in **oceans**. Oceans are made up of **salt water**.

moray eel

Do you know these ocean animals?

1. Which animal looks like a snake?

2. Which animal has a hard shell?

3. Which animal has a big smile?

4. Which animal looks like a parrot?

5. Which animal looks like a tree?

Christmas tree worms

sea turtle

parrotfish

moray eel

dolphin

Answers

1. moray eel
2. sea turtle
3. dolphin
4. parrotfish
5. Christmas tree worm

dolphin

15

Water babies

Some animals live in **fresh water**. Fresh water does not contain a lot of salt. Frogs lay their eggs in ponds. Ponds have fresh water. This pond water is full of frog eggs. There are baby frogs inside the eggs. **Tadpoles** hatch from the eggs. Tadpoles live in water. They grow into frogs.

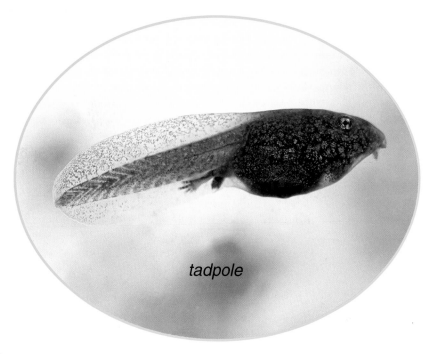

tadpole

frog eggs

Clean and cool

Animals take baths to clean their bodies. They also take baths to keep cool. This elephant is taking a cold shower under a waterfall.

Hippos need to stay in water during the day. Their skin gets very dry in the sun and cracks. Hippos leave the water at night to find food. Tigers like to cool off in water.

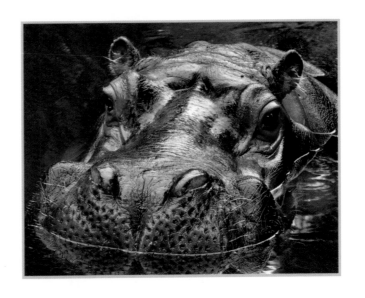

 # Keeping clean

People also need to keep clean to stay healthy. We need to take showers or baths often. We use water to wash ourselves, and the other things we own.

We use water to brush our teeth, too.

We need water to clean our homes. We need water to wash our clothes. This boy is washing dishes. He turned on the tap and filled the sink with water. Name five ways you use water every day.

This girl has washed some towels in the washer. She has dried them in the dryer and folded them.

Water fun

People need water, but most people also love water. Many people swim during the summer. What water games do you play in the pool or at the beach?

People love snow and ice, too.

Snow and ice are frozen water.

We use water in many ways.

Water makes us feel great!

Words to know and Index

clouds
page 7

dew
page 7

ice
pages 7, 23

lakes
page 5

liquids
pages 4, 6, 7

oceans
pages 5, 14-15

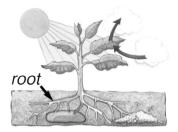

plants
pages 6, 8, 9, 10-11

ponds
pages 5, 16

rain
pages 6, 7

rivers
pages 5, 10

snow
pages 7, 23

Other index words

animals pages 7, 8, 9, 12, 13, 14, 15, 16, 18

fresh water page 16

people pages 8, 12, 20, 22, 23

salt water page 14

24